Super Villains of Persuasion

By Ben Settle

©2019

"Jimmy was the kind of guy that rooted
for bad guys in the movies."
~ Henry Hill, *Goodfellas*

Ben Settle

Table of Contents

Ben Settle

Super Villains of Persuasion

Legal Notices Even Villains
Dare Not Ignore!

This book is Copyright © 2019 Ben Settle
(the "Author"). All Rights Reserved.
Published in the United States of
America. The legal notices, disclosures,
and disclaimers in the front and back of
this book are Copyright © 2009-2011
Law Office of Michael E. Young PLLC,
and licensed for use by the Author. All
rights reserved.

No part of this book may be reproduced
or transmitted in any form or by any
means, electronic or mechanical,
including photocopying, recording, or by
an information storage and retrieval
system — except by a reviewer who may
quote brief passages in a review to be
printed in a magazine, newspaper, blog,
or website — without permission in
writing from the Author. For

information, please contact the Author by e-mail at www.BenSettle.com/contact or by mail at PO Box 2058 Bandon, OR 97411.

For more information, please read the "Disclosures and Disclaimers" section at the end of this book.

First Edition, 2019

Published by Settle, LLC (the "Publisher").

Who is Rood?

Rood is an entrepreneur, author, and self-described "Anti-professional." He is also a master of influence and persuasion and spends all his time in his Lair of Influence writing books, newsletters, and twisted monster novels to finance his world domination plans.

The authorities are aware of Rood's Villainous ambitions. And it amuses him how they can do nothing to stop him, because he masterfully uses a "loophole" in the law that says it's not illegal to plan to take over the world, since no crime has (yet) been committed.

Rood makes no attempt to hide his real identity, his business dealings, or his Mission to force the world to submit to his will. Through his books about persuasion and Villainy, he openly mocks his hero enemies. And the planet's leaders, military, and police are terrified of the coming day when he decides to make his move...

Introduction

-

The Villain's Lair of Influence

"Transylvania is not England.
Our ways are not your ways.
And to you there shall be many
strange things."

— Count Dracula
Bram Stoker's Dracula

Welcome to this second book of my
Success Villains series:

"Super Villains of Persuasion"

The first book *Persuasion Secrets of the
World's Most Charismatic & Influential
Villains* covered the ten most important
fundamentals for building rock-solid
charisma and influence, including:

1. Bow only at the altar of your mission

2. Nix all neediness

3. Pay yourself first

4. Keep a "screw you" fund

5. Shove people off their pedestals

6. Slay your inner nice guy

7. Stake the time vampires

8. Ignore the sheep

9. Submit to patience

  10. Be the Joker

That was the "ground floor" field manual showing men exactly what attributes to have to be attractive, persuasive, respected, influential, wealthy, or to simply be admired by other men & loved by dames.

I liken it to donning the Villain's garb of Charisma:

> The dark cloak, the silver skull-handled cane, the gold signet ring, the concealed bullet-proof Kevlar vest, the villainous sunglasses, etc.

This book is the next phase in your journey:

Super Villains of Persuasion

The figurative construction of your hidden chateau Lair of Influence — strategically placed at the top of a treacherous mountain, complete with a moat, a stocked fine wine cellar, a full staff of henchman to do your bidding, and all the weapons and instruments of conquest you require. A place that will also be just as foreign and hair-raising to your friends and loved ones as the Villainous garb you donned after reading the last book.

But from here you must be comfortable.

As this is where you will position yourself to launch your Influential attacks. And it is also from where you will marshal your forces, and hatch your diabolical plots, putting the world's heroes, the authorities, and your enemies constantly on defense — mindlessly reacting to your every move.

But a word of warning before you begin:

You can learn much from the Villains inside this book without adopting their wicked ways. For just as a surgeon's knife can be used to cut out a tumor and save a life, it can just as easily be used to impale someone through the chest. And that's why it is of utmost importance you use wisdom and ethics when applying what you learn inside this tome. For without those two attributes, the following information will (1) not work nearly as well (and even work *against* you) and (2) almost certainly land you in the same kind of hot spots (such as a prison cell) some of the Villains referenced ultimately ended up in.

So, use these principles wisely, ethically, and to build your Mission. If you do that, nothing can stop you from achieving anything you want:

- Money and wealth
- Power, status, and privilege routinely denied ordinary men

Super Villains of Persuasion

- A "ride-or-die" dame who always has your back
- The loyalty of others
- A higher paying job and professional security
- Greater respect
- A thriving business
- Peace of mind
- Even the world, if that's what you want...

Are you ready to begin?

Then turn the page and start the next phase of your Villainous transfiguration. By the time you've finished reading, you won't even recognize the man you become as a result. And, I dare say, neither will anyone else.

Ben Settle
aka "Rood"

P.S. This book is a happy hunting ground of movie, TV, and comic book story spoilers. You've been warned...

Ben Settle

1
-
The Secret of Possessing Unequaled Greatness

"I'm not a comic book villain. Do you seriously think I would explain my master stroke to you if there were even the slightest possibility you could affect the outcome?"

— Adrian Veidt/Ozymandias
Watchmem

I once read an unusually valuable monologue from the majestic Villain Doctor Doom, analyzing why he is superior to four other major Fantastic Four villains.

Quotes from the short (one page) comic book story include:

"Recently I read a newspaper report referring to me as 'one of the many scientific geniuses who have battled the Fantastic Four.' This is the sort of arrant nonsense I expect from the press. Doom has no peers!"

"Take the Mole Man, for example... he has no real creative genius of his own."

"Kang [The Conqueror — a warlord from the future] is merely a man of his time, while I am a man far in advance of my own."

And, my personal favorite:

"[The Thinker] has succeeded in tapping into almost every computer network on Earth, even the most secret. Except, of course, *mine*. I know this because I have gained access to his."

Super Villains of Persuasion

He then ends his monologue saying he wishes he could actually meet someone who truly challenged him, and who was worthy. But he then quickly dismisses the desire, because the mere thought of it…

Is Unworthy of the Unequaled Greatness That is Doom!

Which brings me to the rub:

Doom's Superior Confidence is what makes him persuasive to those he rules and dangerous to those he battles. It's what make his henchmen fall into line without daring to buck his commands. It's what makes his enemies horrified whenever he hatches his latest plot to rule the world. And, it's this Superior Confidence that…

Makes His Every Word Radiate Influence!

This Superior Confidence is the secret behind the persuasive power of many great Villains, such as:

- Superman's nemesis Lex Luthor
- Asgard's bastard prince Loki

- Narnia's evil dictator Jadis (aka the White Witch)

- John McClane's (*Diehard*) Christmas-time terrorist Hans Gruber

- The X-Men's cunning foe Mr. Sinister

- The Thundercats' arch-fiend Mumm-Rah

- The Pabst Blue Ribbon-loving psychopath Frank Booth (From *Blue Velvet*)

- William "Braveheart" Wallace's sworn enemy King Longshanks

- Aladdin's arch-enemy Jaffar

- The Avengers' most dangerous threat Thanos

- The menacing Col. Nathan R. Jessep (from *A Few Good Men*)

- And the list goes on…

These Villains wield unusually strong powers of influence and persuasion due to the Superior Confidence behind their beliefs that nobody is going to stop them from achieving their Missions. As a result, they have mass influence, loyal henchmen, and an impenetrable "force field" around their egos rendering them virtually immune to doubt, insecurity, anxiety, or the opinions of haters and critics.

After all, do you really think the White Witch would care if someone trolled her online?

Or that Thanos would even entertain listening to someone criticize his political views?

Or that Col. Jessep would be phased in the slightest by a dame who rejects him or snarkily questions his manhood?

Or that Mumm-Rah would feel "offended" by a mean word or insult?

One of the world's greatest persuasion and marketing minds, the great Dan Kennedy, once said people are all walking around, umbilical cord in hand, wanting to plug it in somewhere. Yes, people are looking for someone with confidence and

Ben Settle

boldness to lead, guide, and direct them. To influence them. And in his *NO BS Time Management for Entrepreneurs* book he even admits:

> **"Having a (preferably private) sense of superiority over others is another power-producing edge."**

But he's not the only one who understands this quirk of human nature.

Perhaps the greatest PUA (pick up artist) who ever lived — the mysterious Roissy of Chateau Heartiste — uses this same principle of Superior Confidence to seduce, persuade, and influence the world's most beautiful women. In his infamous *16 Commandments of Poon* (under section XI "Be irrationally self-confident") he reveals the simple secret to gaining that kind of charisma:

> **"No matter what your station in life, stride through the world without apology or excuse."**

Super Villains of Persuasion

To be irrationally self-confident is to have Superior Confidence.

And to have Superior Confidence is to possess powers of persuasion most men can't even imagine. This is why, whatever you do, go forth and do it boldly, with Superior Confidence, and you will be instantly more persuasive.

In time, people who ordinarily would ignore you, will hang on your every word.

Dames who ordinarily would spurn you, will find themselves irresistibly submitting to you.

And people who ordinarily wouldn't pay you any attention or respect, will want to hire you, work for you, fight for you, bleed for you, and even, in some cases...

Die for You!

Superior Confidence is the foundation of your Villainous Lair of Influence.

Without it, the entire structure collapses with the first stiff wind or attack on the outer walls — no matter how strong the

Ben Settle

bricks, how secure the interior, or how impenetrable the gate. If you don't yet think you have Superior Confidence, do not despair. This is a thread that runs through this entire book — intertwined with each principle of persuasion and influence within, all building and compounding on each other chapter by chapter, page by page, and sentence by sentence.

And by the time you're finished?

You too will have this precious attribute not one in a thousand men possesses.

2
-
Persuasion by Pain

"I sense great fear in you,
Skywalker. You have hate. You
have anger. But you don't use
them."

— Count Dooku
Star Wars: Revenge of the Sith

The Villain Erik Killmonger (from *Black Panther*) was just a child living in the slums of Oakland when his father was brutally murdered by his uncle, the King of Wakanda. Child Erik was orphaned by his own family and left completely on his own to figure out his way, with no guardian, no guidance, and no direction. Imagine being dropped off in the middle of a city by your family and told, "good luck!" as a young child, and that is basically what happened to him.

The result?

Well, he could have done what lesser men would do: Given up, despaired, and lived the rest of his life a broken, unsuccessful man, never accomplishing anything.

Instead, he did the opposite and...

Used That Pain to Achieve His Goals!

Including spending years building up his body, his combat experience, and his fighting skills by becoming one of the deadliest assassins and soldiers on the planet... plotting his revenge on those who wronged him... and eventually seizing the Wakandan throne.

Unpleasant as it is, pain is a Villain's greatest asset.

It gives you drive, energy, clarity, purpose, and, yes influence.

Like when Magneto in *X-Men: First Class* watched his mother be killed, and he used that pain to become the X-Men's most dangerous foe and attract many of the world's other Super Villains to join him.

And when Ra's al Ghul in *Batman Begins* lost his wife and daughter and used that pain to rise up to be the leader of the League of Shadows, with a legion of ninjas at his command.

And when Aldrich Killian in *Ironman 3* was rejected and humiliated by Tony Stark, tricked into waiting for him on a cold rooftop in Bern, Switzerland on New Year's Eve, and he used that pain to create the multi-million dollar think tank AIM (Advanced Idea Mechanics), and invent the persona of the dreaded terrorist Mandarin — with whom he influenced and controlled world governments and even the Vice President of the United States.

This goes beyond just Super Villains, though.

Many of history's greatest achievers were motivated by pain to become some of the most influential, charismatic, and persuasive men who ever lived. Take the late "King of Late Night" Johnny Carson, for example. His biographers agree what motivated him to the top of the entertainment world (he was the "celebrity to the celebrities" — with even other "A-List" actors begging for his time and attention) was the pain of his cold, loveless mother never caring about him. It was the same thing that motivated the late Steve McQueen, too. (Who was the highest paid movie star in Hollywood, and also one of the world's best race car drivers).

All of which is why it is foolish and wasteful for a Villain to try to suppress, self-medicate, or rationalize away pain.

Pain is power.

Pain is energy.

And, pain is...

One of the Most Valuable Gifts You Can Possibly Be Given!

Super Villains of Persuasion

Doesn't matter if it's pain from heartbreak, being bullied, social humiliation, parental rejection, mockery, broken ego, regret, betrayal, or anything else.

So, if you have pain, use it.

It can give you the drive and motivation to do things ordinary men can only dream of — in your business, your career, your relationships, or in any other area of your life. The key is to harness and use it without letting it control you. This is where ordinary men go astray. They let their emotions control them, instead of the other way around.

The model is the anti-hero the Hulk.

He is an entity of pure rage and anger. But, when aimed (such as when Bruce Banner "aimed" it at the Abomination in *The Incredible Hulk*)...

That Anger Can Win the Day When All Other Options Have Failed!

The flip-side is, it can also be dangerous and unhealthy to stay in a state of anger.

As Ra's al Ghul warned Bruce Wayne in *Batman Begins*:

"Your anger gives you power. But if you let it, it will destroy you."

This is true both figuratively and literally.

You have to look at your pain like putting on a hat or suit:

You "wear" it when you need it but you take it off when you don't. A Super Villain of Persuasion aims his anger in a focused, purpose-driven (to achieve his Mission) way that creates order in his world — not a blind, raging, furious way that creates chaos and leads to debilitating mistakes.

Do it the right way and your pain will give you powers of persuasion beyond your wildest imagination.

It will give you influence over people who will eagerly want to help you.

And, it will give you a special kind of charisma you can use to go forth and

Super Villains of Persuasion

conquer your enemies and achieve your Mission.

Ben Settle

.

3

-

The Dark Lord of Charisma

"[Sauron] is seeking it, seeking it — all his thought is bent on it."

— Gandalf
The Fellowship of the Ring

Much can be said about why the diabolical vampire Radu Vladislas (from the cult-like following of *Subspecies* B-movies) has such a rabid (even if niche) following. Part of it is his uniquely gruesome looks and demeanor — with his deep, hissing voice and blood constantly drooling and bubbling up out of his mouth every time he speaks. Or his abnormally long fingers that turn into small demonic creatures that carry out his evil commands when he breaks them off.

Or his ability to teleport through shadows to travel far distances before dawn, or to simply appear inside a hapless woman's bedchamber to feed.

Those are all interesting and useful attributes.

But the one attribute that stands out from them all has nothing to do with his looks. Nothing to do with his powers. Nothing even to do with him being a vampire.

This all-powerful attribute of persuasion is known as…

Obsession!

Radu's powers of persuasion come from being obsessed with the things he craves. But not in a needy way. He does it in a dominant, self-assured way, as if the objects and people he desires (namely the Blood Stone, which drips the blood of the saints, and his "play thing" Michelle Morgan — who he made his vampiric fledgling despite her constantly trying to resist his wiles) are his already.

Super Villains of Persuasion

This is a common trait amongst many Villains.

And its power and significance cannot be overstated.

For example, Vox Day once said on his blog:

> **"... consider Sauron, for example. Has anyone ever given any thought to how charismatic he must have been, how inspiring, to not only convince whole kingdoms, whole races, to support his vision for Middle Earth, but even convince some of his most avowed enemies to abandon their fellows and throw in with him?"**

I would argue what gave Sauron his supernatural charisma is the same thing that gave Radu his irresistible powers of influence:

His All-Consuming Obsession!

When used in pursuit of your Mission, Obsession is charismatic.

And, when channeled, it can help you defeat those who are otherwise unbeatable.

Such as the brutal Villain Clubber Lang, who used Obsession to beat and humiliate Rocky — the Heavyweight Champion of the World in *Rocky 3* — with ease. The Motherfucker in *Kick Ass 2* used his Obsession with killing Kick Ass to assemble a team (against his crime boss uncle's commands) of the most dangerous killers on the planet. And, yes, the Dark Lord Sauron used Obsession for finding The One Ring of Power to create an army so powerful, it took the combined might of all the elves, men, wizards, and the very creators of Middle-earth to contend with his will.

But that's just the beginning.

Obsession also means you don't need anything (or anyone) to motivate you. As heavyweight boxing champion Ed Latimore once Tweeted:

"Obsession is the easiest way to accomplish anything. Your decisions are already made, your time already allocated, and your focus at a maximum."

More:

The late, great marketing genius (and master of persuasion & influence) Gary Halbert once wrote in his newsletter (*The Gary Halbert Letter*) about Michael Crichton's best-selling novel *Congo*. Specifically, the part where a group of high level researchers with genius-level IQ's compete for grant money to fund their research projects. There is one character especially persuasive at getting big money grants. And the reason why he is so persuasive is explained in this quote:

"Sometimes it's difficult to tell who is the more brilliant but we look for something more

important: We look for who is the most driven!"

These are just a few reasons why Obsession is known as:

"The Dark Lord of Charisma"

But there is no such thing as equality (a true Villain has no equal…), and this is especially true when it comes to Obsession and who it works for (or against).

In order for Obsession to work for you…

It Must Not Be Done Out of Neediness!

Unfortunately for most men, their Obsessions take the form of wasteful and self-destructive things, like:

- Drugs

- Alcohol abuse

- Partying

- Getting in debt to buy expensive non-assets (cars, clothes, electronics, etc) for "status"

Super Villains of Persuasion

- Chasing dames that disrespect or reject them
- Dopamine addictions (stimulations from entertainment, video games, porn, the internet, etc, where their brains "reward" them for wasting time, and perpetually crave more of the same...)
- Approval seeking
- And the list goes on...

Just like with pain... Obsession will work against you, be unhealthy for you, and utterly sabotage you if you don't invest it correctly. This is why a Super Villain of Persuasion obsesses only over activities that help him achieve his Mission.

Invest your Obsession in that alone, and you will have all the charisma you want.

All the influence you want.

And, yes, all the powers of persuasion you want.

Ben Settle

4
-
The 3-Second "Mind Tweak" That Creates Mass Influence

"The entire time I knew Thanos, he only ever had one goal: To wipe out half the universe."

— Gamora
Avengers: Infinity War

When the Villain Adrian Veight (aka Ozymandius, "The Smartest Man In The World") in *Watchmen* noticed the world sinking into chaos and war... when he saw the doomsday clock was but a minute away from midnight... and when he realized nothing the powers that be, the smooth-talking politicians, or political talking heads could do anything to stop the planet's inevitable nuclear annihilation... there were many things he could have done with his great wealth to stop it.

Such as buying up all the arms manufacturers.

Or bribing the world's politicians and leaders in to making better decisions.

Or possibly even getting himself elected President of the United States and seizing control over the most powerful nation on earth.

But he didn't just want to change the political process.

Or replace the politicians.

Or rule the world.

Instead, he decided to...

Completely Transform Society!

It was the only way to save the world from itself, instead of just applying another temporary "band-aid" of peace treaties and double-talk negotiations.

Super Villains of Persuasion

And he did it by using his vast resources and intellect to create a deadly crisis so unimaginable it would influence the world and its leaders to focus on attacking that threat, instead of attacking each other.

Which bring us to another Super Villains of Persuasion secret:

Thinking Big!

Thinking big let Ozymandius persuade the world's most powerful men to change everything about themselves — including their thinking, their plans, and even the very laws of their own countries. It also persuaded the most powerful man in the world Dr. Manhattan to go against his nature, and kill another Watchman to preserve the peace Ozymandius created.

Thinking big is a staple of a Super Villain of Persuasion's arsenal.

Like when Apocalypse in *X-Men: Apocalypse* decided to destroy all non-mutants by using Charles Xavier's mind to control and eviscerate them using their own nuclear warheads.

Or when Thanos in *Avengers: Infinity War* decided to eradicate poverty, disease, and hunger by wiping out half the universe's population.

Or when Bane during the infamous "Knightfall" comics storyline decided to not just defeat Batman... but completely destroy him — by breaking his back, his legacy, and his spirit.

Or when the Kingpin in Frank Miller's acclaimed *Born Again* storyline discovered Daredevil's secret identity and decided not to merely kill Daredevil, but drive him insane by using his influence to have the IRS seize Matt Murdock's accounts (making him poor), have a police lieutenant testify he saw Murdock pay a witness to perjure himself (making him unable to practice law anymore), and then firebombing his apartment (making him homeless). The Kingpin also made it obvious to Murdock he was the one who did it, further driving Matt Murdock into despair.

More:

In *Rich Dad, Poor Dad*, best-selling author Robert Kiyosaki talks about how the rich and powerful do everything <u>big</u>.

When they win, they win big.

When they lose, they lose big.

But win or lose…

They Do It Big!

Frankly, being a big thinker creates influence by its mere existence.

As your thinking grows bigger, as your plans grow bigger, and as your Mission grows bigger… so does the number of people wanting to listen to you, follow you, and be influenced by you. It's why all the Villains above are always surrounded by loyal henchmen, dames, and "lieutenants" ready to carry out their marching orders.

Best part?

No matter what your position in life, you can do the same thing. All it takes is a 3-second "tweak" in the way you think — where whatever your plans… whatever your ambitions… whatever your goals… you make them bigger.

Enlarge them.

Blow them up as huge as you can.

And then, keep making them bigger, until…

The Size and Scope of Your Plans Takes Even *Your* Breath Away!

That is when you know you're on the right track.

And it is also when you will begin to automatically take your persuasion game to a whole new level where most men are too timid to tread.

5
-
How Even Super Villains of Ill Repute Win Trust

"This isn't Wall Street, this is Hell. We have a little something called Integrity."

- Crowley
King of Hell
Supernatural

The King of Hell/King of the Crossroads demon Crowley (from the TV show *Supernatural*) isn't just a great Super Villain of Persuasion because of his ability to plot, scheme, and lead. But also, because he has the one attribute every Villain must have in order to win and maintain loyalty, trust, and credibility in the eyes of a public programmed to be ruthlessly skeptical of Villains.

And that attribute is…

Integrity!

For instance:

When Crowley makes a deal to steal a soul, his word is his bond. Which is why when one of his crossroad demons started making greedy pacts to get souls by breaking his rules, he canceled the scoundrel demon's deals (even though Crowley would have benefited from them) and took him back to hell to torment him, while declaring:

"You make a deal, you keep it."

However, this isn't just limited to Crowley.

Many Super Villains of Persuasion have their own (even if warped) code of Integrity.

Such as the Red Hood in *Batman: Under the Red Hood* — where the Red Hood seized control of the mafia and Gotham City's crime bosses. He allowed crime and required a cut of the profits. But, the line was drawn at selling drugs to children.

It was also the case with Don Corleone in *The Godfather* — who abhorred people who made promises they couldn't keep, valued family over everything, and also prohibited selling drugs.

And also with the maniacal Tuco in *Better Call Saul* — whose sense of Integrity made him open to being negotiated with by Jimmy McGill, who talked Tuco down from killing and burying a couple con artists (who tried to con Tuco's grandmother) in the desert... to merely breaking one leg each, instead.

There was also the violent gangster Jimmy Conway in *Goodfellas* — who paid everyone for their assistance, regardless of how small the task, and refused to rat his friends out no matter what. (Even if he had no qualms about whacking them out of paranoia...)

And so, it is with many other Super Villains such as Loki, Lex Luthor,

Thanos, Magneto, and even Skeletor who escorted a couple kids through Eternia and didn't let evil befall them. (Then declared after saving one of them, "I am NOT nice!") Frankly, even hardened criminals in America's worst prisons show a certain level of Integrity by the way they are quick to attack and kill child molesters imprisoned with them.

Yes, the above villains and criminals may very well be vile scumbags.

But, they also have a sense (even if tenuous) of Integrity.

And that Integrity is what makes them in some ways — their evil, sociopathic, and often megalomaniacal actions notwithstanding — trustworthy, credible, and, when needed…

More Persuasive Than Many of the Heroes And So-Called "Good Guys."

And here's something else:

Having Integrity even in trivial matters gives you influence. Take, for example, the great marketing teacher Dan Kennedy again, who declared in his *NO BS Time Management* book:

"First of all, being punctual gives you the right—the positioning—to expect and demand that others treat your time with the utmost respect. You cannot reasonably hope to have others treat your time with respect if you show little or no respect for theirs. So, if you're not punctual, you have no leverage, no moral authority. But the punctual person gains that advantage over staff, associates, vendors, clients, everybody."

And make no mistake, being punctual is a form of Integrity.

As is telling the truth.

Being ethical in your deals.

Never going back on your word (no matter how beneficial it would be to you).

Not skimming off the top even if you can "get away" with it.

Doing what you say you'll do, when you say you'll do it.

And delivering nothing but your best effort and work.

Moral (or immoral, depending on the Villain…) of the story?

Being consistent in your Integrity wins you the trust of other men and Villains alike.

And That Trust Means More *Influence* Over Other Men and Villains Alike, Too.

So, in everything you do, do it with Integrity.

It's one of the few things that not only weeds out the merely average men from great men, but also weeds out the merely great men from the bona fide Super Villains of Persuasion.

6
-
Donning the Mask of Authority

*"Nobody cared who I was until
I put on the mask."*

— Bane
The Dark Knight Rises

Believe it or not, the above quote has one of the most valuable lessons in Villain history about persuasion embedded within.

How so?

Because many great (even iconic) Villains were originally ignored, disrespected, mocked, and shunned. But, the second they put their masks on...

They Instantly Received All the Attention, Respect, and Influence

Ben Settle

They Desired!

Case in point:

- **Darth Vader from the *Star Wars* movies** — originally Anakin Skywalker couldn't even muster up enough clout to have a voice on the Jedi Council after being appointed a seat by the Chancellor (with the other council members insulting him by refusing to recognize his membership). But after he put the Darth Vader mask on, he became a powerful and fearsome presence all the Jedi feared, and all the inhabitants throughout the galaxy obeyed.

- **Puzzle from *The Chronicles of Narnia: The Last Battle*** — who was a mere talking donkey in a land full of talking animals. Nobody thought him special, or worthy of respect and loyalty. But, when he and his friend (the devious talking Ape Shift) found a lion skin left over by a hunter, Shift made Puzzle wear it to impersonate the lion Aslan, creator of Narnia. The result? Almost overnight, Puzzle went from being a nobody, to the single most influential animal in the country.

- **Jason Voorhees from the *Friday the 13th* movies** — most people have no clue what he looked like before donning his signature hockey mask. But after he wore it, he became one of the most frightening and iconic Villains ever recorded. Jason's mask was so impactful, even Freddy Krueger in *Freddy vs Jason* used Jason to "remind" the children in the neighborhood he used to haunt about him, so they'd believe in his existence again, which would allow him to escape hell and take physical form.

- **The Reverend Jonathan Whirley** — the evil leader of the Pagan gang in the movie *Dragnet*. Sans his mask, he was a mild-mannered reverend, with a soft, unassuming nature. But when donning the Pagan mask, he became a sinister figure who sacrificed virgins to a giant snake and committed crimes around the city.

- **Jonathan Crane** — the Scarecrow in *Batman Begins* was just a non-physically imposing figure in his day job as a lawyer. But when he put on his mask (and especially when he released his fear toxin) he became one of the most unforgettable figures people saw. (And, sometimes, the *last* person they saw…)

But this phenomenon doesn't just apply to physical masks.

In the movies and comics, actual masks are necessary. And usually, the scarier and more menacing the better. But here in the real world, a Villain's Mask is subtler, less obvious, and can potentially make you far more persuasive and influential than any physical mask can.

In fact, when you don the Villain's Mask correctly…

You Will Create an Authoritative Personality

People Won't Be Able to Resist Following!

It doesn't matter if you are a complete nobody now.

Or even if you have the personality of Homer Simpson.

To give you an example, there was once a series of short Q&A documentaries with various Hollywood directors. One of the featured directors was John Singleton who directed the acclaimed *Boyz 'n the Hood.* And one of the things John Singleton talked about was how certain world-famous celebrities had to create their own larger-than-life personas in order to stand out in the industry. One of which was 2Pac. According to John Singleton, 2Pac wasn't naturally as eccentric and dramatic as his celebrity persona was. Yes, it was essentially him and his personality. But it was exaggerated.

And the same goes for Ice Cube, too, as well as several other people he'd worked with.

And you know what?

After dealing with some of the most popular personalities in the marketing and business world, I can testify that creating your own larger-than-life personality not only makes you way more interesting, influential, and persuasive… but also extremely unique, too. Especially since most men will never do it. And the reason why they won't do it is because…

They Are Frozen with Fear
At the Mere Thought
Of Even Just Being Themselves!

Can you imagine that?

People are too scared to even be their authentic selves.

(Much less exaggerate their personalities like 2Pac and others).

To give you an idea of how widespread this fear is, podcasters and influential leaders in the marketing world have invited me to teach their audiences how to be "authentic."

Yes, it's gotten so bad...

Men Literally Have to be *Taught* How to be Themselves!

That's why most men live their entire lives fearing what others will think or say about them. Their culture, their teachers, their friends, their family, even their parents have programmed them to fear being themselves, to avoid rejection, and to resist saying, doing, or believing in anything that causes pushback, personal attacks, and being challenged.

The result?

The vast majority of men have become incapable of being noticed.

(Much less respected.)

And this is good news for a Villain who sacs up and conquers this fear. Because when you know how to take your authentic personality and augment it (ala 2 Pac, Ice Cube, etc.)…

You Will Have No Competition!

Not in business.

Not in your professional life.

And certainly not when competing for dames, respect, money, recognition, opportunity, privilege, and all the other perks enjoyed by Villains unafraid of doing what it takes to stand out from the bleating herd.

But you may be wondering, how do you don this Mask?

Especially if you've gone your entire life paralyzed by fear of it?

The answer is simple:

**Take Your Personality
And Exaggerate It a Few Notches.**

If there's an attribute about your personality you enjoy (especially a so-called "negative" attribute) don't hide and suppress it.

Super Villains of Persuasion

Own it.

Blow it up.

And, have fun *reveling* in it.

For instance, I have made it no mystery to my website readers, customers, podcast listeners, and whenever I speak publicly (or privately) about the contempt I have for large crowds. I would much rather hang out alone (like most Villains, I quite enjoy my own company...) than with a group of 30+ people obnoxiously competing to be heard.

So, I don't bother trying to convince people I'm social or fun.

Instead, I do the exact opposite:

I accept and brag about it when people accuse me of being crotchety, antisocial, and "Grinch-like." The last thing I do is hide that negative aspect of my personality.

I Run with It!

That's where the whole elBenbo persona (the Mask I have donned in business) came from. It's an exaggeration of an aspect of my personality one of my ex-girlfriends used to complain about.

But, a couple warnings:

First, there can only be one Bane. One Darth Vader. One Joker. One Scarecrow. One Jason Voorhees. One Pennywise the Clown, and so on.

So, don't try to copy another Villain's mask.

Your Mask Must Be Unique to You And Your Personality.

To copy is to be a fraud.

And to be a fraud is to be completely inauthentic.

Plus, trying to be (for example) another Bane, will just water down the Mask for you both. (While pissing Bane off…)

And the second warning?

Your personality should be lovable. My elBenbo Mask is (I like to think, at least) somewhat lovable. He's <u>not</u> likeable, necessarily. In fact, many people hate him. But, he is lovable. And if you paint yourself as an evil, abusive sociopath with no conscience, it could work against you.

So, when it comes to donning your Villains Mask, remember:

If you have a flaw, don't hide it, run with it.

Make it noticeable and unique.

And then own it.

That's how you create a Villainous Mask that transcends you and still be 100% authentic. Do that, and you'll have a mask people either love or hate, with zero indifference.

And that's what you want.

Because at the end of the day...

Indifference Is the Death of All Persuasion and Influence!

So, don your Villains Mask of Authority, and do it soon.

Only then, a true Super Villain of Persuasion can you be...

Ben Settle

7

-

The Sexiest Influencer of Them All

*"If you're good at something,
never do it for free."*

— The Joker
The Dark Knight

In *Sin City: A Dame to Kill For*, the Villainous femme fatale Ava Lord uses an extremely potent principle that can make any Villain more persuasive, more respected, and more influential… while also granting you a peace of mind and sense of security most people will never know.

Here's what happened:

Ava's Mission was to have her wealthy husband killed, and frame her ex-lover Dwight for the deed, so she could get all her husband's wealth. But to do so, she did not try to use money (she had lots of it). Nor did she try to use brute force (she had a driver who could have done that). Instead, she used a far more powerful force at her disposal.

And, that force was…

Specialization!

In her case, she used her sensuality and her sexuality.

Those were her Specializations that allowed her to persuade and influence everyone from her driver to beat up and protect her from her enemies, to getting her ex-lover to kill her husband, to even getting the cop assigned to her to break protocol and eventually kill his partner (and then himself) to help protect Ava and her secret.

That is the power of Specialization.

Everyone loves a specialist.

Everyone trusts a specialist.

And, everyone is susceptible to a specialist's persuasive wiles.

Super Villains of Persuasion

This is true whether it's a specialist who does great good (such as an oncologist who specializes in helping children suffering and dying from cancer) or whether it's a specialist who does great evil (like the depraved rapist Dr. Larry Nassar who specialized in helping athletes for the USA Gymnastics team, and molested dozens of those patients at his office and gym…)

Frankly, Specialization is such a powerful tool of persuasion and influence…

It Works Even if You Do Everything Else Wrong!

For example:

Many years ago, there was a video of an interview with a nerdy-looking guy who was a world champion (i.e. specialist) at a certain video game. This is a guy who dressed like a schlub, looked like a schlub, and lived the life of a video-game playing schlub. The kind of guy most women would not even glance at and would most likely laugh at. (Or just ignore and hope he doesn't try to speak to them). I'm talking about someone who spends his entire life in front of a screen and is about as naturally charming as Beavis & Butthead.

Except, for when it came to his craft.

Most video game nerds display zero charisma, power, or confidence. And they are far more likely to mow a Villain's lawn or fetch his lunch, than to be a Villain themselves. Yet, in this interview, this nerd... this *specialist*... not only had the body language, confidence, and swag of a Villain, but he had a beautiful girlfriend who clearly adored and respected him on his arm, too.

This simply doesn't happen to video game nerds.

But it did to this one.

And the reason why is because...

He Is the Best in the World at What He Does!

Super Villains of Persuasion

That's the influential and persuasive power of Specialization.

In business, Specialization lets you charge more for what you sell (a brain surgeon charges far more than a general practitioner). It automatically gives you more prestige, status, and respect (a lawyer who specializes in helping Hollywood celebrities gets more money, prestige, status, and respect than a lawyer who takes on anyone as a client). And it makes you instantly have more credibility and believability in whatever it is you specialize in —

Whether You Deserve It or Not!

In your personal life, if you're a specialist, you are the one everyone asks for help with regarding whatever you specialize in.

In your professional life, if you're a specialist, you will have the kind of iron-clad job security no piece of paper from a University can even come close to giving you.

And in your business life, if you're a specialist, you will automatically be in the all-coveted "catbird seat" — the place to where money and clients effortlessly flow. In fact, in some cases…

People Will Even Hire
You on the Spot!

And, do it without price, salary, or fee objection.

All because you specialize in what they want done.

So, if you want to be more persuasive, specialize.

Just as Dr. Curt Connors (the Lizard in *The Amazing Spiderman*) specialized in genetic biology and had the trust of the Chief of Police and school authorities… just as Wilson Fisk (The Kingpin in the Netflix *Daredevil* series) specialized in all things business, and thus had the good faith and admiration of an entire city's political leaders… just as Saruman the White in the *Lord of The Rings* stories specialized in magic and was the highest ranked wizard with the attention and respect of the entire White Council… just as the Joker in *The Dark Knight* was the only one the ultra-violent mob factions in Gotham City had enough faith in to get the job of killing Batman done (and paid him half their fortunes to do it)… if you specialize in that which you want to be known for, you will have all the prestige, influence, and persuasive hold you wish.

And, in many cases, you won't even have to do much to earn it.

It will simply fall in your lap.

Such is the raw power of Specialization.

Ben Settle

8
-
The Diabolical Goal-Setting Method that Never Fails

"We too are on a quest to better ourselves, evolving toward a state of perfection."

- Borg Queen
Star Trek: First Contact

In the novel *Forrest Gump*, Forrest becomes an astronaut, goes to outer space, and crashes on an island in New Guinea. There he meets a tribe of cannibals, led by a Villain named Big Sam. Big Sam is Yale-educated, and even pokes fun at Forrest's stint at Harvard.

The Villain also teaches Forrest how to play chess.

And Forrest — who has a natural talent for chess — continually beats Big Sam.

Each time they play, Big Sam gets closer to beating Forrest. And with each game, it becomes clear Big Sam intends to eat Forrest when he eventually does win. Inevitably, Forrest falls into a trap and knows he's going to lose and has to think up a way to escape.

Anyway, here is the punchline:

Big Sam isn't just frightening because he wants to eat Forrest.

He's Frightening Because He Knows He's Going to Win!

And Forrest knows it, too, which makes him needy.

(After all, he *needs* to win or become lunch…)

Big Sam, on the other hand, doesn't get needy or emotional, because he doesn't need to win like Forrest does. If he did, he'd have been the mistake-prone one, and probably would never win.

Question is, how did Big Sam create this mistake-creating neediness in Forrest?

Answer:

Instead of focusing on winning (which he couldn't control), Big Sam focused on getting better at the game (which he could control), and that...

Made Winning Inevitable For the Villainous Cannibal!

And so it is with many great Villains.

Such as the Borg in *Star Trek*.

Their goal isn't to take over the galaxy, it's to constantly better themselves, which allows them to assimilate more worlds, continually grow stronger, and capture more ground. There is zero neediness or worrying about if they will win. To them, it is inevitable. And so they focus on getting better, stronger, and more "perfect."

Another example is the Villain Glass from *Unbreakable*.

His life's Mission is to find the hero he is — by destiny — supposed to battle. And to find this hero he spends his life committing terrorist attacks to draw the hero out, without worrying or stressing if he will find him, knowing it's inevitable.

The point?

Whether it's Big Sam wanting to eat Forrest, the Borg taking over the galaxy, or Glass finding the hero, these Villains all have one thing in common with many of the great negotiators, marketers, salesman, and other great influencers:

Outcome Independence!

Here's what that means in "plain English":

Don't focus on what you can't control. (The outcome.)

Instead, focus on what you <u>can</u> control. (The process.)

So, if you want to lose a bunch of weight, don't focus on losing 50 lbs. (which you can't control). Set a goal to eat right each day, to exercise regularly, to be more active, to work on balancing your hormones (if they are out of whack), to get better sleep, and to lay off the booze and sugar.

Unlike the number on the scale, these are all things you can control.

And focusing on the things you can control (and not on the things you can't)…

Completely Eliminates Anxiety, Fear, and Frustration!

And, makes reaching your goal inevitable.

Here's another example:

If you want to find a hot, pleasant, "ride-or-die" woman who wants nothing more in life than to keep your belly full and your balls empty, don't focus on "finding that woman" (which you can't control). Focus on your Mission, consistently going to the gym, improving your confidence (specializing is a good way to do this...), working on your business, chatting up women you find interesting, not being needy, observing what the guys who already have the kind of woman you want do (as comedian Dante Nero says, "don't ask the deer how to hunt it, ask the hunter"), regularly going to places the kind of woman you want is likely to spend time at, and being the highest value man you can be.

One more example:

If you want to make six or seven figures per year, don't focus on making the six or seven figures (which you can't control). Focus on consistently making yourself a better, more "promotable" employee. Or (if you have your own business) consistently sending attractive offers to receptive leads, with back-end offers and systems in place. Or to consistently save and invest your money, while continually educating yourself about investing.

Whatever your ultimate goals are, the message is clear:

Super Villains of Persuasion

Whether it's finding a woman, a better job, having more money, or anything else...

Focus on What You Can Control, And Not on What You Can't Control.

This is how you create true Outcome Independence.

It also helps build Superior Confidence (since it ensures victory 100% of the time).

And because it attracts people to you, seeking out your help, and making them more open to your influence... it will make you a Super Villain of Persuasion, too.

Ben Settle

9
-
How Villains Create Luck out of Thin Air

"I lived my entire life waiting for this moment. I trained, I lied, I killed just to get here. I killed in America, Afghanistan, Iraq... I took life from my own brothers and sisters right here on this continent! And all this death just so I could kill you."

- Erik Killmonger
— *Black Panther*

My *Persuasion Secrets of the World's Most Charismatic & Influential Villains* book revealed how Patience was like a "superpower" of influence. It's one of the rarest attributes of modern man. Frankly, a Villain with Patience is a Villain who has control over other men —

Including Having Control Over Men Who Themselves Have Control Over Other Men!

And guess what?

This all-powerful attribute has a *cousin* just as rare and just as powerful, exemplified by the devious Villain Amy Dunne in *Gone Girl*. To see what this great superpower of persuasion is, study her monologue (midway through the movie) outlining the steps she took to accomplish her Mission to fake her death and convince the world her husband murdered her:

- She spent months writing 300+ separate diary entries telling a narrative to the police — from the first time she met her husband until the present. The narrative showed a husband she was madly in love with, but who abused her, cheated on her, and scared her so much she tried to buy a gun.

- To solidify her narrative, she inquired about buying a gun with the local meth dealer, knowing he wouldn't sell it to her (since it wasn't his specialty). And also knowing full well the cops would ask him about her, and that he'd remember her.

- She befriended and made a "local idiot" her unknowing accomplice by patiently learning all the details of her boring life and telling her fake stories to gain her sympathy (for later on) about her husband's temper.

- She secretly created a bunch of traceable money troubles by charging online gambling, golf clubs, a big TV, gadgets, and other expenses in her husband's name.

- She had her husband bump up her life insurance policy, so he'd get even more money should she meet an untimely demise, further adding to a motive for killing her.

- She bought a cheap, beat up car on Craigslist with cash — completely untraceable — to secretly slip out of town in.

- She faked a pregnancy to gain the public's sympathy, knowing America loves a pregnant woman. She did it by tricking her local idiot friend (who was pregnant) into giving her some of her urine by (1) coaxing the toilet and preventing it from flushing (2) serving her local idiot a lot of lemonade so she'd have to pee (3) stealing the pee (4) then taking a pregnancy test at the doctor's, making being pregnant part of her permanent legal medical record.

- When the morning of her "death" came (their 5th wedding anniversary) she told her husband to go to a specific spot (that was far away from people, so there would be no alibi as to his whereabouts that day) to "think about the marriage."

- Right after he left, she meticulously staged the crime scene using knowledge she gained by studying police detective procedure from books and case studies — leaving just enough mistakes to lead the cops to automatically be suspicious of foul play by her husband.

- Part of the staging was taking her own blood via an IV and splashing it all over the floors, as if she had a mortal head wound.

- She then cleaned it up sloppily (like a man in a panic would).

- Finally, she burned the 300+ entry diary just enough where it looked like her husband tried to destroy it but failed, while making sure it was found in a spot the cops would look.

As you can see, it took more than mere patience to pull this off. It also required the assistance of another attribute used by many Super Villains of Persuasion called:

"Superior Preparation"

If Patience is the *cloak* of your Villainous garb, then Superior Preparation is the secret *study* in your hidden mountain chateau Lair of Influence from where you plot and hatch your master plan. It's oftentimes the one thing that makes the difference between a Villain being caught and imprisoned or getting away with the spoils, with no possibility of being found, discovered, or captured.

Other great Villains who have used Superior Preparation include:

- **Erik Killmonger in *Black Panther*** — who spent a lifetime using Superior Preparation to hatch his plan to claim the Wakandan throne and get his revenge.

- **Zemo in *Captain America 3: Civil War*** — where he (successfully) plotted the destruction of the Avengers by pitting them against each other.

- **Lex Luthor in *Batman v Superman*** — every decision, move, and action he made for almost two years straight was aimed at manipulating Batman into fighting Superman.

Super Villains of Persuasion

- **The demon Toby in the _Paranormal Activity_ movies** — who (over multiple generations) persuaded entire families of people to give him what he wanted (the soul of the next male born in their family line) in exchange for giving them what they wanted (money and supernatural power). Incidentally, Toby the demon brilliantly tapped into what Bernard Baruch (the man called "the most persuasive man of the 20th century") said was his "big secret" of persuasion on his deathbed:

"Find Out What People Want And Show Them How to Get it."

Villains know persuasion doesn't happen in a vacuum.

All great achievements take Superior Preparation.

And that's why Superior Preparation has been used, taught, and practiced by many of the greatest minds in the arena of influence. Including military leaders, executives of billion-dollar corporations, and the most respected & successful advertising, marketing, legal, and political minds who ever lived.

The most prepared Villains always wins.

It is the next best thing to casting a magic spell on yourself that...

Gives You the Influence and Control To Achieve Anything You Want!

Plus, there's this, too:

A Villain with Superior Preparation has zero competition.

After all, Superior Preparation takes work. It takes diligence. And, it takes persistence. These are traits ordinary men are too impatient, too lazy, and too unmotivated to cultivate. Which is why when you experience massive success using Superior Preparation, the first thing people will accuse you of is being...

"Lucky"

And in a way, they are right.

Super Villains of Persuasion

After all, what is luck if not being *prepared* for opportunities?

But that is also why when the wagging tongues of ordinary men speak of your success they will almost surely begin calling you lucky and making excuses for their own failures and lack of ambition. When that happens, smirk and nod, realizing they are the people most ripe for being influenced and persuaded to do your bidding.

For to paraphrase Loki when he came to Earth in *The Avengers*:

Lesser men were made to be ruled over... by a Villain.

Ben Settle

10

-

The Superpower That Bends People Helplessly to Your Will

"...this is not some common lunatic. The type of intestinal fortitude it must take... to keep a man bound for a full year. To connect tubes to his genitals. To sever his hand and use it to plant fingerprints. He's methodical and exacting, and worst of all, he's patient."

— Detective Somerset
— *Se7en*

In the movie *Se7en* the frighteningly Villainous John Doe commits a number of elaborate and grisly murders over seven days, that are as intricate as they are methodical. And the detectives working the case soon realize they are dealing with a serial killer who is carefully targeting people representing each of the seven deadly sins.

For example:

- A man was forced to eat until his stomach ruptured (gluttony)

- A defense attorney was killed by having a literal pound of flesh taken from him (greed)

- A drug dealer and child molester was emaciated alive (sloth)

- A man was forced to kill a prostitute by raping her with a custom-made, bladed strap-on (lust)

- A model's face is mutilated by Doe; while she was given the option to call for help and be disfigured, or commit suicide by taking pills (pride)

Even more bone-chilling than the crimes is the attribute it took to make everything come together — in just the right way, at just the right times, with just the right impact needed to get the desired result.

And that attribute is none other than…

Willpower!

Willpower is the throne room in the Super Villain's Lair of Influence.

Whether it be psychopathic Villains like John Doe in *Se7en*… mentally tormented Villains like Harvey Dent in *The Dark Knight* (who carried out his revenge on the mob, Commissioner Gordon, and Batman simultaneously, all while in agonizing pain from having half his face seared off)… or money-obsessed Villains like El Capitan in *Ducktales* (who spent centuries seeking the map to his lost gold, living that long only through sheer force of will)… Willpower is…

The King Attribute Possessed by Super Villains of Persuasion!

Indeed, one must have abundant Willpower to even be a Villain.

For without Willpower, how can you have Patience? Or have Superior Preparation? Or resist the multiple daily temptations to ignore your sense of Integrity when presented the opportunity to "get away" with giving in to those temptations? Or put in the often mind-numbingly tedious and boring effort to master a skill to Specialize in? Or have the Superior Confidence it takes to control your emotions when tested by dames, disobedient henchmen, or random circumstances beyond your control?

That's why, like it or not, for Villains, Willpower is…

A Non-Negotiable Requirement!

A Villain without Willpower is not truly a Villain any more than a hero without someone to save is a hero.

The one cannot exist without the other.

At the very least, you need more Willpower than those you wish to influence.

Super Villains of Persuasion

The good news is, anyone can have strong Willpower just as anyone can have strong biceps. Because, like your biceps, Willpower is a muscle. And like any muscle, it can be strengthened (with use) or weakened (with non-use). It can grow (with resistance) or it can shrink (with zero resistance). And, it can help you overpower and destroy (with rigorous exercise), or it can atrophy and become useless (if never used at all).

For most, Willpower is the latter, and by far...

The Least Used Muscle of All!

If you doubt this, observe popular culture.

There are countless ads, infomercials, books, so-called scientific articles, and websites selling diet products and philosophies touting how they require no Willpower, saying it is not reliable, and how they can show you how to get what you want without it.

To ordinary men, Willpower is something to avoid and mock that holds them back.

But to a Villain, Willpower is something to pursue and celebrate that lets you…

Bend Others to Your Will!

A Villain also knows it comes first, since it makes all the other Superpowers of Persuasion work.

As FJ Shark (author of *How to be The Jerk Women Love*) once wrote:

> **"Willpower is everything. It can create, destroy, dissolve, unite, conquer, anything. Control over money, control over others, all of that is secondary. The triumph of the will is the greatest accomplishment of humanity, the pinnacle of sentient achievement."**

This is why Villains with strong Willpower are unnaturally influential.

People just know — by the way you look, the way you speak, the way you move,

even the way you write — you are
mentally and emotionally stronger than
them (even if not necessarily physically).
People are attracted to mental and
emotional toughness over physical
toughness. All the great Villains and
leaders of men have always had
exceptionally stronger Willpower than
their enemies, subordinates, henchmen,
dames, soldiers (who, incidentally, have
always been physically stronger than the
Villains who commanded them, further
proving the superiority of Willpower over
any other muscle), and anyone else they
want to influence and persuade.

But what about you?

Is Your Willpower Strong…
Or Is it Flaccid?

Answer with 100% Integrity:

Does your Willpower help you persuade
and influence?

Or does it repel and create indifference?

If the answer is the latter, then I propose
a test. A test guaranteed (if you do it to

the letter) to strengthen your Willpower beyond that of probably everyone you know. And that test is to pick the one vice you lack the most Willpower to control, and that is holding you back from accomplishing your Mission…

And "Fast" From it For 30 Full Days!

For example:

If you're addicted to fapping, cease doing it for 30 days.

If your vice is sitting on the couch all day wasting your life watching TV, then throw your couch and TV away for 30 days and do something productive with that time instead (i.e. pursue your Mission).

If you're a heavy drinker, no alcohol for 30 days.

If you smoke, no nicotine for 30 days.

If you are addicted to junk food, no sugar for 30 days.

And the list goes on.

Super Villains of Persuasion

Whatever your vice is (the above are only a few examples)... especially the one you are having the hardest time controlling and that is holding you back from achieving your Mission... you abstain from it for 30 days.

But before you begin, a few things to think about:

1. If you fail at any time during your 30 days you start over again from day one. No whining, complaining, or excuses. The goal is to strengthen your Willpower, not coddle it.

2. You will likely be excited to start, only to hate everything a day later. This is where Integrity comes in again. Character, Integrity, Superior Confidence, Patience, and of course Willpower... are strengthened beyond that of ordinary men every time you follow through on a decision long after the excitement of the moment has passed.

3. FJ Shark said something else about Willpower you should think about constantly during your 30-day test:

"The key to success in any endeavor is not to work when you are motivated; it is to work when you are Unmotivated."

Truer words have nary been spoken.

It's easy to do anything when you're motivated, excited, and energetic.

Not so much when you're tired, bored, and distracted.

So, if you have the guts, do this 30-day test. And do it cheerfully, knowing it will not only help create an indomitable Willpower, but also with the knowledge that doing it is 100% in your control — with complete Outcome Independence.

To put it bluntly:

The Only Way to Lose Is If You Quit!

So, start your 30-day test today.

Super Villains of Persuasion

Don't put it off until tomorrow or the first of the month or New Year's.

Do it now, as soon as you close this book, and you will begin creating a strong kind of Willpower your enemies will tremble at, and those you wish to influence will respond to.

I hope you enjoyed this book detailing the ten of the most potent traits possessed by the Super Villains of Persuasion. And, even more importantly, I hope you implement this information, and that it makes you not only a better person, but a more persuasive and influential Villain, too.

For an ongoing "Villainous" education in email marketing, copywriting, selling, and persuasion, go here next:

www.BenSettle.com

Ben Settle

Dastardly Disclosures & Disclaimers

All trademarks and service marks are the properties of their respective owners. All references to these properties are made solely for editorial purposes. Except for marks actually owned by the Author or the Publisher, no commercial claims are made to their use, and neither the Author nor the Publisher is affiliated with such marks in any way.

Unless otherwise expressly noted, none of the individuals or business entities mentioned herein has endorsed the contents of this book.

Limits of Liability & Disclaimers of Warranties

Because this book is a general educational information product, it is not a substitute for professional advice on the topics discussed in it.

The materials in this book are provided "as is" and without warranties of any kind either express or implied. The Author and the Publisher disclaim all warranties, express or implied, including, but not limited to, implied warranties of merchantability and fitness for a particular purpose. The Author and the Publisher do not warrant that defects will be corrected, or that any website or any server that makes this book available is free of viruses or other harmful components. The Author does not warrant or make any representations regarding the use or the results of the use of the materials in this book in terms of their correctness, accuracy, reliability, or otherwise. Applicable law may not allow the exclusion of implied warranties, so the above exclusion may not apply to you.

Under no circumstances, including, but not limited to, negligence, shall the

Super Villains of Persuasion

Author or the Publisher be liable for any special or consequential damages that result from the use of, or the inability to use this book, even if the Author, the Publisher, or an authorized representative has been advised of the possibility of such damages. Applicable law may not allow the limitation or exclusion of liability or incidental or consequential damages, so the above limitation or exclusion may not apply to you. In no event shall the Author or Publisher total liability to you for all damages, losses, and causes of action (whether in contract, tort, including but not limited to, negligence or otherwise) exceed the amount paid by you, if any, for this book.

You agree to hold the Author and the Publisher of this book, principals, agents, affiliates, and employees harmless from any and all liability for all claims for damages due to injuries, including attorney fees and costs, incurred by you or caused to third parties by you, arising out of the products, services, and activities discussed in this book, excepting only claims for gross negligence or intentional tort.

You agree that any and all claims for gross negligence or intentional tort shall be settled solely by confidential binding arbitration per the American Arbitration Association's commercial arbitration rules. All arbitration must occur in the municipality where the Author's principal place of business is located. Arbitration fees and costs shall be split equally, and you are solely responsible for your own lawyer fees.

Facts and information are believed to be accurate at the time they were placed in this book. All data provided in this book is to be used for information purposes only. The information contained within is not intended to provide specific legal, financial, tax, physical or mental health advice, or any other advice whatsoever, for any individual or company and should not be relied upon in that regard. The services described are only offered in jurisdictions where they may be legally offered. Information provided is not all-inclusive and is limited to information that is made available and such information should not be relied upon as all-inclusive or accurate.

For more information about this policy, please contact the Author at the e-mail address listed in the Copyright Notice at the front of this book.

IF YOU DO NOT AGREE WITH THESE TERMS AND EXPRESS CONDITIONS, DO NOT READ THIS BOOK. YOUR USE OF THIS BOOK, PRODUCTS, SERVICES, AND ANY PARTICIPATION IN ACTIVITIES MENTIONED IN THIS BOOK, MEAN THAT YOU ARE AGREEING TO BE LEGALLY BOUND BY THESE TERMS.

Affiliate Compensation & Material Connections Disclosure

This book may contain hyperlinks to websites and information created and maintained by other individuals and organizations. The Author and the Publisher do not control or guarantee the accuracy, completeness, relevance, or timeliness of any information or privacy policies posted on these linked websites.

You should assume that all references to products and services in this book are made because material connections exist between the Author or Publisher and the providers of the mentioned products and services ("Provider"). You should also assume that all hyperlinks within this book are affiliate links for (a) the Author, (b) the Publisher, or (c) someone else who is an affiliate for the mentioned products and services (individually and collectively, the "Affiliate").

The Affiliate recommends products and services in this book based in part on a good faith belief that the purchase of such products or services will help readers in general.

The Affiliate has this good faith belief because (a) the Affiliate has tried the product or service mentioned prior to recommending it or (b) the Affiliate has researched the reputation of the Provider and has made the decision to recommend the Provider's products or services based on the Provider's history of providing these or other products or services.

The representations made by the Affiliate about products and services reflect the Affiliate's honest opinion based upon the facts known to the Affiliate at the time this book was published.

Because there is a material connection between the Affiliate and Providers of products or services mentioned in this book, you should always assume that the Affiliate may be biased because of the Affiliate's relationship with a Provider and/or because the Affiliate has received or will receive something of value from a Provider.

Perform your own due diligence before purchasing a product or service mentioned in this book.

The type of compensation received by the Affiliate may vary. In some instances, the Affiliate may receive complimentary products (such as a review copy), services, or money from a Provider prior to mentioning the Provider's products or services in this book.

In addition, the Affiliate may receive a monetary commission or non-monetary compensation when you take action by clicking on a hyperlink in this book. This includes, but is not limited to, when you purchase a product or service from a Provider after clicking on an affiliate link in this book.

Purchase Price

Although the Publisher believes the price is fair for the value that you receive, you understand and agree that the purchase price for this book has been arbitrarily set by the Publisher. This price bears no relationship to objective standards.

Due Diligence

You are advised to do your own due diligence when it comes to making any decisions. Use caution and seek the advice of qualified professionals before acting upon the contents of this book or any other information. You shall not consider any examples, documents, or other content in this book or otherwise provided by the Author or Publisher to be the equivalent of professional advice.

The Author and the Publisher assume no responsibility for any losses or damages resulting from your use of any link, information, or opportunity contained in this book or within any other information disclosed by the Author or the Publisher in any form whatsoever.

YOU SHOULD ALWAYS CONDUCT YOUR OWN INVESTIGATION (PERFORM DUE DILIGENCE) BEFORE BUYING PRODUCTS OR SERVICES FROM ANYONE OFFLINE OR VIA THE INTERNET.

THIS INCLUDES PRODUCTS AND
SERVICES SOLD VIA HYPERLINKS
EMBEDDED IN THIS BOOK.

Super Villains of Persuasion

CPSIA information can be obtained
at www.ICGtesting.com
Printed in the USA
FSHW020900050119
54848FS